AUTHOR: HEARTBREAK CLINIC
ILLISTRATOR: ANNE BISMONTE

HEARTBREAK CLINIC

How To Live Your Life While Single

We can all agree that being single isn't as easy as it sounds. It can be even more stressful, especially during Holidays. All in all, it's not all doom and gloom-no siree! There are certain perks to being single. For one, you don't have to share your bed with anyone. But I must say, being single could sometimes drain your energy if you want to be in a relationship.

Regardless, we need to learn how to live without worrying about our relationship status. I know, I know; it's easier said than done. Well, if you are trying to continue living no matter your current relationship status, then you've come to the right place.

Below, we will discuss all the tips that could help you keep the ball rolling in your single life and still manage to be happy.

With that in mind, let's get started, shall we?

Get Involved in Engaging Activities

The best way to always have a happy life is by focusing on how you spend your time. That's because how you spend your time has a lot to contribute to your mindset. You can very well be lonely and unhappy in a relationship. That said, you must focus your energy on what you do daily.

Being single means, you have full control of your life, and now is the perfect time to pick up an engaging sport or exercise routine. Most people prefer hitting the gym and getting back in shape. At the same time, others try to take care of their minds and bodies differently, for instance, yoga and meditation. All in all, try to find a sport that's engaging and will develop your body and mind.

That will help you enjoy the moment and appreciate all that's happening around you. We all tend to think that happiness comes after love, but that's not the case. You can find a way to be happy and single; having someone else to experience the joy of life will only be the icing on the cake. More importantly, the more comfortable you are alone, the more likely you will attract an amazing partner.

A simple hobby should help pre-occupy any negative thoughts that you might have. That said, find out what kinds of activities you like and start working on them, even if it's playing chess or checkers.

Do Whatever You Want on Your Terms

Most of the time, when people are in a relationship, they tend to feel lost in the relationship. And the most significant contributor being the fact that you now stop doing things independently.

You have to consider your partner in everything you do, which can sometimes impact your happiness. See that one thing you loved to do, but it always annoyed your ex? Well, now that you are single, guess what? You have the chance to do whatever you want on your terms.

There will be no one on your case telling you what you need to do or not. So, you can decide to have ice-cream for dinner if that's what makes you happy. Or you can even take over the other side of the closet and watch those girly TV shows shamelessly without someone judging your life choices. Even if you want to sing silly songs as you dance around the house, then go ahead.

In short, when you are single, it's your chance to let loose and enjoy being you.

Confidence Boost

Without a doubt, confidence is attractive.

That said, whenever you are alone, remember that there's confidence that is always deep inside you. Therefore, you only need to tap into it and show it even when you are not alone.

Most times, we tend to rely on our partners to boost our confidence levels, and it's a bit challenging to find your confidence level when you are alone. Thankfully, being single gives you the chance to find your inner strength and confidence. The best part is that this could manifest into an even stronger level of confidence. When you are alone, you will get the chance to self-reflect, and that could breed confidence.

It's impossible to have a great relationship when there is some part within that is not being attended to, so do the work to become the best version of you. Once you've found that inner confidence alone, it will trickle into every other relationship you have in your life.

Above all, now that you've understood what you need, it will be easier for you to connect with someone in a romantic way. Therefore, self-reflection also helps to attract the right future partner.

Pursue Your Goals

Most people expect that relationships will make them a better person and hence they can pursue their goals. Well, that's not true. As much as a relationship gives you the confidence to chase your dreams, it shouldn't be the only reason you want to be successful. We all have ambitions that we can pursue before getting into a relationship. Sometimes it doesn't have to be a big goal; it can be something as simple as not wearing eyelash extensions. Yes, you heard that right! Makeup is a way to express ourselves to the world, but there are those of us who use makeup to hide away.

You don't need a relationship to tell you that you are beautiful. All you have to do is look in the mirror and tell yourself that you love what you see. Then after that, you can apply makeup with a different goal. We all know how hard it can be to start a family alone. Being a single parent is not an easy task. But if your goal is to be a parent, then being single shouldn't stop you. If you are up for the job, then you will do everything in your power to become a parent, whether you are single or not.

I mean, we live in the 21st century. You can adopt or even get a donor to help if having a baby is your heart's desire.

Past Lessons

I understand why you might be skeptical about starting a new relationship because of a bad experience in your past. However, the only reason why you are afraid of falling in love again is that your history is your trap. Instead of focusing on all the pain your past relationship brought, you can look at the lessons learned!

I'm sure you learned a lot from your experience, which will help you not repeat the same mistake. It's time to forget about your ex and move on to find your happiness. I'm not saying that it will be easy; I'm saying that it will be worth it. All it takes is one step at a time.

Start focusing on the lessons and the rest you will figure out as you continue with your life.

Not All Thoughts Are Facts

Another problem you are likely to face when you are single is identifying facts from thoughts. There's a high chance you are single because of the negative thoughts in your mind such as, 'I can't find love' or 'all the good ones are taken.' That's not entirely true.

Once you have a positive mind, you will likely find the right partner for you. More importantly, you don't have to look for someone to love. For some reason, your positive energy will attract the right partner for you. The trick is to be content with what you have and continue hoping for a better day in the future. That said, when you start having such ideas in your mind, remind yourself that not everything that runs through your head is a reality.

It's not written in stone, and you can change your future if only you believe it. More importantly, not all thoughts we have are the truth. Sometimes our minds create thoughts to protect us from handling the truth or facing it. Therefore, you need to be careful about dealing with any negative thought that crosses your mind. Instead of choosing to believe the negative thinking, note it down on a piece of paper.

The next step is to forget about it and develop a pattern of positive thoughts.

Money Mindset

Most people in relationships will say one of the perks is that both partners share their financial burdens and responsibilities. But according to Financial experts, being single incentivizes you to be more financially responsible and frugal.

Having a partner is very expensive. You have to plan for dates, Anniversaries, Christmas gifts, birthday gifts, and more dates. In short, there are lots of responsibilities that require money when in a relationship. On the other hand, when you are single, no one in your life will push you to incur expenses that were not in your budget. That means that you get to max out your credit card alone, or you could decide to maximize your savings.

When you are single, you get to be more resourceful since you are not relying on sharing expenses with someone else.

That, in turn, natures your financial responsibility, which will be useful not only for your life but also your career.

Fall in Love with Yourself First

When you are seeing someone, it's easy to forget to invest in your relationship with yourself. But your relationship with yourself is equally important, so why don't you invest in it and make it the best you have?

All the special treatment you would give your partner or the treatment you would expect from your partner, why not do it yourself? You have been giving too much love to the world, and now that you are single, it's time to turn it inward.

Cultivate Compassion

Cultivating self-compassion is a beautiful practice that you need to nature with yourself. It doesn't matter where you are at currently with yourself, love. Start with self-compassion, and it changes how you view yourself and other people in your life. Self-compassion will drive you to have more self-acceptance in your life.

You will cultivate more body acceptance; When you are single, you get ample time to spend time with your body and find ways to appreciate it. You could even create rituals that will help you take care of your body by eating nourishing foods or moving your body in ways that make you feel more vibrant.

For some people, body acceptance could be something as simple as spending time putting on their favorite lotion. That helps them take time with each part of their body, expressing what they love most about that area.

Also, you can try to get in touch with your more feminine side. Probably you could take a long bath then wear your favorite lingerie. That will help to accentuate your feminine side and discover your sensual side.

New Friends

Every person needs some support system in their life. And now that you are single, you can now choose the friends in your life. You can have friends of both genders, take pictures together, go out together, and enjoy life. These new connections may allow you to grow a relationship with a tribe of supporters.

As we all know, sometimes it can be hard to foster such friendships when you are in a relationship. Sometimes, you might even have friends but never have the chance to spend time with them. It can be exhausting to split your attention.

But now that you are single, you don't have to split attention. You only need to be there for the people that matter in your life and be there for them, too, when they need you. There's a certain sense of fulfillment that comes with being there for the people that matter in your life.

AFFIRMATIONS

I give up the habit of criticizing myself
My life purpose keeps me motivated

I believe in the power of positivity
I find new ways to feel good
I choose to surround myself with supportive and good people
I am becoming more resilient each day
I am doing my best and that is enough
I am intelligent
I release negative thoughts
and emotions
I deserve a partner who loves and respects me
I can get through anything
I choose a peaceful and calm spirit
My days are filled with happiness and blessing
I am in charge of my thoughts
I am going to reach every goal i set for myself
I am comfortable with I am
I am open to limitless possibilities

AFFIRMATIONS

I am exactly where i am meant to be
I trust that all that I need comes to me when needed
I only compare myself to myself
I am attracting great success and prosperity
I radiate happiness and well-being
I am powerful enough to overcome negativity
I have unlimited potential
I can create my own positive energy
I feel blessed today
Mistakes are only lessons to be learned
There is nothing I am afraid of
I choose hope over fear
I can push through whatever life throws at me
I trust the process of life
I enjoy working on improving myself
The only approval i need is mine
I have the power to change
I am learning more about myself
I am moving forward
I am looking forward to all the changes life may bring
I listen to my body
My future is full of infinite possibilities
I am worthy of great things

ACTIVITY WORKSHEETS

Live a Full
Life While Single

WHAT DOES SELF-LOVE LOOK LIKE?

So often people think external factors influence their happiness, but that's simply not true. Happiness comes from within when you love yourself. Use this worksheet to help build and strengthen your awareness of self-love.

What does self-love look like for you:

Benefits I will receive from loving myself:

WHAT DOES SELF-LOVE LOOK LIKE?

So often people think external factors influence their happiness, but that's simply not true. Happiness comes from within when you love yourself. Use this worksheet to help build and strengthen your awareness of self-love.

Negative thoughts that keep me from being happy:

Ways I can be kind to myself:

ELIMINATE TOXIC RELATIONSHIPS

Becoming the best version of yourself will require you to let go of people and things that may not be good for you. Think for a moment about the times when you felt exhausted, stressed, overwhelmed, or defeated. Are there some people who contributed to these negative feelings? Is there a consistent pattern of negative behavior or negative characteristics?

What are some behaviors you cannot accept or tolerate? What boundaries do you need to set?

SELF-CARE IDEAS

Sometimes it can be super easy to think about what we can do to be there, love, support, and encourage others, but we can feel a bit lost or maybe not know where to get started with self-care. One of the most significant investments you will ever make is investing in yourself. Take some time to think about how you would like to care for your mind, body, and soul.

MIND

Read motivational books
Accomplish a small goal
Read inspirational quotes
Listen to Podcast
Color mandala
Learn a new skill
Brain dump
Clean out your closet
Create a vision board
Meditation
Declutter your home

BODY

Try a new recipe
Drink water
Get a message
Get plenty of sleep
Practice yoga
Exercise
Get some sun
Take a relaxing bath
Stretch

SOUL

Take a nature walk
Listen to music
Buy fresh flower
Watch the sun rise
Write a gratitude journal
Burn your favorite candle
Dress up for no reason
Bake something

SELF-CARE GOALS

DUE DATE: _____

Goals:

Motivation:

Action Plan:

SELF-CARE ROUTINE

Now that you have come up with some self-care ideas and set a few goals. Take some time to plan for success. Take some time to write down how you will take care of the amazing skin you are in because when you take care of yourself - you feel better inside and out.

AM/PM	DAILY	WEEKLY	MONTHLY
Cleansing			
Exfoliating			
Toning			
Moisturising			
Sunscreen			
Serum			
Eye Cream			
Spa Treatment			

I am a beautiful soul:

_____
_____
_____

MONTHLY SELFCARE CALENDAR

Self-care may not happen daily, but it is essential to make it a part of your on-going weekly or monthly routine. Take some time to think about how you would like me to take care of you in the upcoming days.

SUN	MON	TUE	WED	THURS	FRI	SAT

WEEKLY EXERCISE TRACKER

Exercise improves mental health by reducing anxiety and negative mood and by improving self-esteem. Exercise also alleviates symptoms such as low self-esteem and social withdrawal.

Get up and get your body moving because when you look good, you feel great; what are you going to do to get your body moving in the upcoming days?

	EXERCISE ROUTINE	DURATION
Monday		
Tuesday		
Wednesday		
Thursday		
Friday		
Saturday		
Sunday		

STOP THE NEGATIVE TALK

NEGATIVE THOUGHT	POSITIVE THOUGHT
I'm a failure	I'm learning as I go
I'm taking advantage of	I'm trusting
I'm tired	I'm getting the rest I need
I'm not attractive	I'm beautiful as I am
I'm no good at times	I need more practice
I'm bored	I love new challenges
I can't	I can
I'm not sure	I'll figure it out

DAILY PLANNER: Monday

Date : _____
Sleep Hours : _____
Mood :

😢 😟 😐 🙂 😊
very sad somewhat sad neutral somewhat happy very happy

Today I'm grateful for: _____

EXERCISE	TIME

BREAKFAST	LUNCH	DINNER	SNACK

Life lessons & what I've learned from yesterday :

_____
_____

DAILY PLANNER: Tuesday

Date : _____
Sleep Hours : _____
Mood :

😟 😦 😐 🙂 😊
Very sad Somewhat sad Neutral Somewhat happy Very happy

Today I'm grateful for: _____

EXERCISE	TIME

BREAKFAST	LUNCH	DINNER	SNACK

Life lessons & what I've learned from yesterday :

_____
_____

DAILY PLANNER: Wednesday

Date : _____
Sleep Hours : _____
Mood :

😟 😕 😐 🙂 😊
very sad somewhat sad neutral somewhat happy very happy

Today I'm grateful for: _____

EXERCISE	TIME

BREAKFAST	LUNCH	DINNER	SNACK

Life lessons & what I've learned from yesterday :

_____
_____

DAILY PLANNER: Thursday

Date : _____
Sleep Hours : _____
Mood :

😣 😟 😐 🙂 😊
Very sad Somewhat sad Neutral Somewhat happy Very happy

Today I'm grateful for: _____

EXERCISE	TIME

BREAKFAST	LUNCH	DINNER	SNACK

Life lessons & what I've learned from yesterday :

_____
_____

DAILY PLANNER: Friday

Date : _____
Sleep Hours : _____
Mood :

😟 😦 😐 🙂 😊
very sad somewhat sad neutral somewhat happy very happy

Today I'm grateful for: _____

EXERCISE	TIME

BREAKFAST	LUNCH	DINNER	SNACK

Life lessons & what I've learned from yesterday :

_____

_____

DAILY PLANNER: Saturday

Date : _____
Sleep Hours : _____
Mood :

😟 😕 😐 🙂 😊
very sad somewhat sad neutral somewhat happy very happy

Today I'm grateful for: _____

EXERCISE	TIME

BREAKFAST	LUNCH	DINNER	SNACK

Life lessons & what I've learned from yesterday :

_____

_____

DAILY PLANNER: Sunday

Date : _____
Sleep Hours : _____
Mood :

😟 😕 😐 🙂 😊
very sad   somewhat sad   neutral   somewhat happy   very happy

Today I'm grateful for: _____

EXERCISE	TIME

BREAKFAST	LUNCH	DINNER	SNACK

Life lessons & what I've learned from yesterday :
_____
_____

DAILY PLANNER: Monday

Date : _____
Sleep Hours : _____
Mood :

😫 😟 😐 🙂 😄
Very Sad Somewhat Sad Neutral Somewhat Happy Very Happy

Today I'm grateful for: _____

EXERCISE	TIME

BREAKFAST	LUNCH	DINNER	SNACK

Life lessons & what I've learned from yesterday :

_____
_____

DAILY PLANNER: Tuesday

Date :
Sleep Hours :
Mood :

😞 😟 😐 🙂 😊
very sad   somewhat sad   neutral   somewhat happy   very happy

Today I'm grateful for:

EXERCISE	TIME

BREAKFAST	LUNCH	DINNER	SNACK

Life lessons & what I've learned from yesterday :

DAILY PLANNER: Wednesday

Date : _____
Sleep Hours : _____
Mood :

😠 😟 😐 🙂 😊
very sad   somewhat sad   neutral   somewhat happy   very happy

Today I'm grateful for: _____

EXERCISE	TIME

BREAKFAST	LUNCH	DINNER	SNACK

Life lessons & what I've learned from yesterday :

_____

_____

DAILY PLANNER: Thursday

Date : _____
Sleep Hours : _____
Mood :

😟　　😕　　😐　　🙂　　😊
very sad　somewhat sad　neutral　somewhat happy　very happy

Today I'm grateful for: _____

EXERCISE	TIME

BREAKFAST	LUNCH	DINNER	SNACK

Life lessons & what I've learned from yesterday :

_____

_____

HEARTBREAK CLINIC

DAILY PLANNER: Friday

Date : _____
Sleep Hours : _____
Mood :

😟 😕 😐 🙂 😊
Very sad Somewhat sad Neutral Somewhat happy Very happy

Today I'm grateful for: _____

EXERCISE	TIME

BREAKFAST	LUNCH	DINNER	SNACK

Life lessons & what I've learned from yesterday :

_____
_____

DAILY PLANNER: Saturday

Date : _____
Sleep Hours : _____
Mood :

😟 😕 😐 🙂 😊
very sad   somewhat sad   neutral   somewhat happy   very happy

Today I'm grateful for: _____

EXERCISE	TIME

BREAKFAST	LUNCH	DINNER	SNACK

Life lessons & what I've learned from yesterday :

_____
_____

DAILY PLANNER: Sunday

Date : _____
Sleep Hours : _____
Mood :

😟 😕 😐 🙂 😊
Very sad   Somewhat sad   Neutral   Somewhat happy   Very happy

Today I'm grateful for: _____

EXERCISE	TIME

BREAKFAST	LUNCH	DINNER	SNACK

Life lessons & what I've learned from yesterday :

_____
_____

DAILY PLANNER: Monday

Date : _____
Sleep Hours : _____
Mood :

😞   🙁   😐   🙂   😊
very sad   somewhat sad   neutral   somewhat happy   very happy

Today I'm grateful for: _____

EXERCISE	TIME

BREAKFAST	LUNCH	DINNER	SNACK

Life lessons & what I've learned from yesterday :

_____

_____

DAILY PLANNER: Tuesday

Date : _____
Sleep Hours : _____
Mood :

😫 😟 😐 🙂 😊
Very Sad   Somewhat Sad   Neutral   Somewhat Happy   Very Happy

Today I'm grateful for: _____

EXERCISE	TIME

BREAKFAST	LUNCH	DINNER	SNACK

Life lessons & what I've learned from yesterday :

_____

_____

HEARTBREAK CLINIC

DAILY PLANNER: Wednesday

Date : _____
Sleep Hours : _____
Mood :

😟   😞   😐   🙂   😊
very sad   somewhat sad   neutral   somewhat happy   very happy

Today I'm grateful for: _____

EXERCISE	TIME

BREAKFAST	LUNCH	DINNER	SNACK

Life lessons & what I've learned from yesterday :

_____
_____

DAILY PLANNER: Thursday

Date : _____
Sleep Hours : _____
Mood :

😫 😟 😐 🙂 😊
Very Sad Somewhat Sad Neutral Somewhat Happy Very Happy

Today I'm grateful for: _____

EXERCISE	TIME

BREAKFAST	LUNCH	DINNER	SNACK

Life lessons & what I've learned from yesterday :

_____
_____

DAILY PLANNER: Friday

Date : _____
Sleep Hours : _____
Mood :

☹️ 🙁 😐 🙂 😃
very sad   somewhat sad   neutral   somewhat happy   very happy

Today I'm grateful for: _____

EXERCISE	TIME

BREAKFAST	LUNCH	DINNER	SNACK

Life lessons & what I've learned from yesterday :
_____
_____

DAILY PLANNER: Saturday

Date : _____
Sleep Hours : _____
Mood :

😟 😕 😐 🙂 😊
Very sad Somewhat sad Neutral Somewhat happy Very happy

Today I'm grateful for: _____

EXERCISE	TIME

BREAKFAST	LUNCH	DINNER	SNACK

Life lessons & what I've learned from yesterday :

_____
_____

DAILY PLANNER: Sunday

Date : _____
Sleep Hours : _____
Mood :

😠 😟 😐 🙂 😄
very sad somewhat sad neutral somewhat happy very happy

Today I'm grateful for: _____

EXERCISE	TIME

BREAKFAST	LUNCH	DINNER	SNACK

Life lessons & what I've learned from yesterday :

_____

_____

DAILY PLANNER: Monday

Date : _____
Sleep Hours : _____
Mood :

😣   😟   😐   🙂   😊
very sad   somewhat sad   neutral   somewhat happy   very happy

Today I'm grateful for: _____

EXERCISE	TIME

BREAKFAST	LUNCH	DINNER	SNACK

Life lessons & what I've learned from yesterday :

_____
_____

DAILY PLANNER: Tuesday

Date : _____
Sleep Hours : _____
Mood :

😟　　😕　　😐　　🙂　　😊
very sad　somewhat sad　neutral　somewhat happy　very happy

Today I'm grateful for: _____

EXERCISE	TIME

BREAKFAST	LUNCH	DINNER	SNACK

Life lessons & what I've learned from yesterday :
_____
_____

DAILY PLANNER: Wednesday

Date :
Sleep Hours :
Mood :

😟 😕 😐 🙂 😃
Very Sad   Somewhat Sad   Neutral   Somewhat Happy   Very Happy

Today I'm grateful for:

EXERCISE	TIME

BREAKFAST	LUNCH	DINNER	SNACK

Life lessons & what I've learned from yesterday :

DAILY PLANNER: Thursday

Date : _____
Sleep Hours : _____
Mood :

😟 😕 😐 🙂 😊
very sad somewhat sad neutral somewhat happy very happy

Today I'm grateful for: _____

EXERCISE	TIME

BREAKFAST	LUNCH	DINNER	SNACK

Life lessons & what I've learned from yesterday :

_____

_____

DAILY PLANNER: Friday

Date : _____
Sleep Hours : _____
Mood :

😠 😟 😐 🙂 😀
Very sad Somewhat sad Neutral Somewhat happy Very happy

Today I'm grateful for: _____

EXERCISE	TIME

BREAKFAST	LUNCH	DINNER	SNACK

Life lessons & what I've learned from yesterday :

_____

_____

DAILY PLANNER: Saturday

Date : _____
Sleep Hours : _____
Mood :

😢　　😟　　😐　　🙂　　😄
very sad　somewhat sad　neutral　somewhat happy　very happy

Today I'm grateful for: _____

EXERCISE	TIME

BREAKFAST	LUNCH	DINNER	SNACK

Life lessons & what I've learned from yesterday :

_____
_____

DAILY PLANNER: Sunday

Date : _____
Sleep Hours : _____
Mood :

😖 😟 😐 🙂 😊
Very sad   Somewhat sad   Neutral   Somewhat happy   Very happy

Today I'm grateful for: _____

EXERCISE	TIME

BREAKFAST	LUNCH	DINNER	SNACK

Life lessons & what I've learned from yesterday :

_____
_____

DAILY PLANNER: Monday

Date : _____
Sleep Hours : _____
Mood :

😦 😟 😐 🙂 😊
very sad somewhat sad neutral somewhat happy very happy

Today I'm grateful for: _____

EXERCISE	TIME

BREAKFAST	LUNCH	DINNER	SNACK

Life lessons & what I've learned from yesterday :

_____
_____

DAILY PLANNER: Tuesday

Date : _____
Sleep Hours : _____
Mood :

😠 😟 😐 🙂 😊
Very sad Somewhat sad Neutral Somewhat happy Very happy

Today I'm grateful for: _____

EXERCISE	TIME

BREAKFAST	LUNCH	DINNER	SNACK

Life lessons & what I've learned from yesterday :

_____

_____

DAILY PLANNER: Wednesday

Date : _____
Sleep Hours : _____
Mood :

☹ ☹ 😐 🙂 😊
very sad   somewhat sad   neutral   somewhat happy   very happy

Today I'm grateful for: _____

EXERCISE	TIME

BREAKFAST	LUNCH	DINNER	SNACK

Life lessons & what I've learned from yesterday :
_____
_____

DAILY PLANNER: Thursday

Date :
Sleep Hours :
Mood :

😞　😟　😐　🙂　😊
Very Sad　Somewhat Sad　Neutral　Somewhat Happy　Very Happy

Today I'm grateful for:

EXERCISE	TIME

BREAKFAST	LUNCH	DINNER	SNACK

Life lessons & what I've learned from yesterday :

DAILY PLANNER: Friday

Date : _____
Sleep Hours : _____
Mood :

😢 😟 😐 🙂 😊
very sad somewhat sad neutral somewhat happy very happy

Today I'm grateful for: _____

EXERCISE	TIME

BREAKFAST	LUNCH	DINNER	SNACK

Life lessons & what I've learned from yesterday :

_____
_____

DAILY PLANNER: Saturday

Date : _____
Sleep Hours : _____
Mood :

😠 😟 😐 🙂 😊
very sad   somewhat sad   neutral   somewhat happy   very happy

Today I'm grateful for: _____

EXERCISE	TIME

BREAKFAST	LUNCH	DINNER	SNACK

Life lessons & what I've learned from yesterday :

_____

_____

DAILY PLANNER: Sunday

Date :
Sleep Hours :
Mood :

very sad   somewhat sad   neutral   somewhat happy   very happy

Today I'm grateful for:

EXERCISE	TIME

BREAKFAST	LUNCH	DINNER	SNACK

Life lessons & what I've learned from yesterday :

DAILY PLANNER: Monday

Date :
Sleep Hours :
Mood :

☹️ 😕 😐 🙂 😊
Very Sad Somewhat Sad Neutral Somewhat Happy Very Happy

Today I'm grateful for:

EXERCISE	TIME

BREAKFAST	LUNCH	DINNER	SNACK

Life lessons & what I've learned from yesterday :

DAILY PLANNER: Tuesday

Date : _____
Sleep Hours : _____
Mood :

😟　　😔　　😐　　🙂　　😊
very sad　somewhat sad　neutral　somewhat happy　very happy

Today I'm grateful for: _____

EXERCISE	TIME

BREAKFAST	LUNCH	DINNER	SNACK

Life lessons & what I've learned from yesterday :

_____

_____

DAILY PLANNER: Wednesday

Date : _____
Sleep Hours : _____
Mood :

😠 😟 😐 🙂 😊
very sad   somewhat sad   neutral   somewhat happy   very happy

Today I'm grateful for: _____

EXERCISE	TIME

BREAKFAST	LUNCH	DINNER	SNACK

Life lessons & what I've learned from yesterday :

_____

_____

DAILY PLANNER: Thursday

Date : _____
Sleep Hours : _____
Mood :

😠 😟 😐 🙂 😄
very sad somewhat sad natural somewhat happy very happy

Today I'm grateful for: _____

EXERCISE	TIME

BREAKFAST	LUNCH	DINNER	SNACK

Life lessons & what I've learned from yesterday :

_____
_____

DAILY PLANNER: Friday

Date : _____
Sleep Hours : _____
Mood :

😫   🙁   😐   🙂   😃
Very Sad   Somewhat Sad   Neutral   Somewhat Happy   Very Happy

Today I'm grateful for: _____

EXERCISE	TIME

BREAKFAST	LUNCH	DINNER	SNACK

Life lessons & what I've learned from yesterday :

_____

_____

DAILY PLANNER: Saturday

Date : _____
Sleep Hours : _____
Mood :

😟 😕 😐 🙂 😄
very sad   somewhat sad   neutral   somewhat happy   very happy

Today I'm grateful for: _____

EXERCISE	TIME

BREAKFAST	LUNCH	DINNER	SNACK

Life lessons & what I've learned from yesterday :

_____
_____

DAILY PLANNER: Sunday

Date : _____
Sleep Hours : _____
Mood :

😟　　😕　　😐　　🙂　　😊
Very Sad　Somewhat Sad　Neutral　Somewhat Happy　Very Happy

Today I'm grateful for: _____

EXERCISE	TIME

BREAKFAST	LUNCH	DINNER	SNACK

Life lessons & what I've learned from yesterday :

_____
_____

DAILY PLANNER: Monday

Date :
Sleep Hours :
Mood :

very sad   somewhat sad   neutral   somewhat happy   very happy

Today I'm grateful for:

EXERCISE	TIME

BREAKFAST	LUNCH	DINNER	SNACK

Life lessons & what I've learned from yesterday :

DAILY PLANNER: Tuesday

Date : _____
Sleep Hours : _____
Mood :

😫 😟 😐 🙂 😄
Very Sad   Somewhat Sad   Neutral   Somewhat Happy   Very Happy

Today I'm grateful for: _____

EXERCISE	TIME

BREAKFAST	LUNCH	DINNER	SNACK

Life lessons & what I've learned from yesterday :

_____
_____

DAILY PLANNER: Wednesday

Date : _____
Sleep Hours : _____
Mood :

😟 😕 😐 🙂 😊
very sad   somewhat sad   neutral   somewhat happy   very happy

Today I'm grateful for: _____

EXERCISE	TIME

BREAKFAST	LUNCH	DINNER	SNACK

Life lessons & what I've learned from yesterday :

_____
_____

DAILY PLANNER: Thursday

Date : _____
Sleep Hours : _____
Mood :

😠 😟 😐 🙂 😊
Very Sad Somewhat Sad Neutral Somewhat Happy Very Happy

Today I'm grateful for: _____

EXERCISE	TIME

BREAKFAST	LUNCH	DINNER	SNACK

Life lessons & what I've learned from yesterday :

_____
_____

DAILY PLANNER: Friday

Date: _____
Sleep Hours: _____
Mood:

😢 😟 😐 🙂 😊
very sad   somewhat sad   neutral   somewhat happy   very happy

Today I'm grateful for: _____

EXERCISE	TIME

BREAKFAST	LUNCH	DINNER	SNACK

Life lessons & what I've learned from yesterday:

_____
_____

DAILY PLANNER: Saturday

Date :
Sleep Hours :
Mood :

☹ ☹ 😐 🙂 😊
Very Sad   Somewhat Sad   Neutral   Somewhat Happy   Very Happy

Today I'm grateful for:

EXERCISE	TIME

BREAKFAST	LUNCH	DINNER	SNACK

Life lessons & what I've learned from yesterday :

DAILY PLANNER: Sunday

Date : _____
Sleep Hours : _____
Mood :

😞 😟 😐 🙂 😊
very sad somewhat sad neutral somewhat happy very happy

Today I'm grateful for: _____

EXERCISE	TIME

BREAKFAST	LUNCH	DINNER	SNACK

Life lessons & what I've learned from yesterday :

_____
_____

DAILY PLANNER: Monday

Date : _____
Sleep Hours : _____
Mood :

😟 😕 😐 🙂 😊
Very sad Somewhat sad Neutral Somewhat happy Very happy

Today I'm grateful for: _____

EXERCISE	TIME

BREAKFAST	LUNCH	DINNER	SNACK

Life lessons & what I've learned from yesterday :

_____
_____

DAILY PLANNER: Tuesday

Date :
Sleep Hours :
Mood :

😞 😟 😐 🙂 😊
very sad   somewhat sad   neutral   somewhat happy   very happy

Today I'm grateful for:

EXERCISE	TIME

BREAKFAST	LUNCH	DINNER	SNACK

Life lessons & what I've learned from yesterday :

DAILY PLANNER: Wednesday

Date : _____
Sleep Hours : _____
Mood :

  ☹️   🙁   😐   🙂   😊
Very sad Somewhat sad Neutral Somewhat happy Very happy

Today I'm grateful for: _____

EXERCISE	TIME

BREAKFAST	LUNCH	DINNER	SNACK

Life lessons & what I've learned from yesterday :

_____

_____

DAILY PLANNER: Thursday

Date : _____
Sleep Hours : _____
Mood :

☹️ 😟 😐 🙂 😄
very sad   somewhat sad   neutral   somewhat happy   very happy

Today I'm grateful for: _____

EXERCISE	TIME

BREAKFAST	LUNCH	DINNER	SNACK

Life lessons & what I've learned from yesterday :
_____
_____

HEARTBREAK CLINIC

DAILY PLANNER: Friday

Date : _____
Sleep Hours : _____
Mood :

Very Sad | Somewhat Sad | Neutral | Somewhat Happy | Very Happy

Today I'm grateful for: _____

EXERCISE	TIME

BREAKFAST	LUNCH	DINNER	SNACK

Life lessons & what I've learned from yesterday :

_____

_____

DAILY PLANNER: Saturday

Date : _____
Sleep Hours : _____
Mood :

😟 😕 😐 🙂 😊
very sad   somewhat sad   neutral   somewhat happy   very happy

Today I'm grateful for: _____

EXERCISE	TIME

BREAKFAST	LUNCH	DINNER	SNACK

Life lessons & what I've learned from yesterday :

_____

_____

HEARTBREAK CLINIC

DAILY PLANNER: Sunday

Date : _____
Sleep Hours : _____
Mood :

😢 😟 😐 🙂 😄
Very sad Somewhat sad Neutral Somewhat happy Very happy

Today I'm grateful for: _____

EXERCISE	TIME

BREAKFAST	LUNCH	DINNER	SNACK

Life lessons & what I've learned from yesterday :

_____
_____

DAILY PLANNER: Monday

Date : _____
Sleep Hours : _____
Mood :

😠   🙁   😐   🙂   😊
Very sad   Somewhat sad   Neutral   Somewhat happy   Very happy

Today I'm grateful for: _____

EXERCISE	TIME

BREAKFAST	LUNCH	DINNER	SNACK

Life lessons & what I've learned from yesterday :

_____
_____

DAILY PLANNER: Tuesday

Date : _____
Sleep Hours : _____
Mood :

😠 😟 😐 🙂 😃
Very Sad   Somewhat Sad   Neutral   Somewhat Happy   Very Happy

Today I'm grateful for: _____

EXERCISE	TIME

BREAKFAST	LUNCH	DINNER	SNACK

Life lessons & what I've learned from yesterday :

_____
_____

DAILY PLANNER: Wednesday

Date :
Sleep Hours :
Mood :

😠 😟 😐 🙂 😄
very sad somewhat sad neutral somewhat happy very happy

Today I'm grateful for:

EXERCISE	TIME

BREAKFAST	LUNCH	DINNER	SNACK

Life lessons & what I've learned from yesterday :

DAILY PLANNER: Thursday

Date : _____
Sleep Hours : _____
Mood :

😢   🙁   😐   🙂   😊
Very sad   Somewhat sad   Neutral   Somewhat happy   Very Happy

Today I'm grateful for: _____

EXERCISE	TIME

BREAKFAST	LUNCH	DINNER	SNACK

Life lessons & what I've learned from yesterday :

_____
_____

HEARTBREAK CLINIC

DAILY PLANNER: Friday

Date : _____
Sleep Hours : _____
Mood :

😟 😦 😐 🙂 😊
very sad   somewhat sad   neutral   somewhat happy   very happy

Today I'm grateful for: _____

EXERCISE	TIME

BREAKFAST	LUNCH	DINNER	SNACK

Life lessons & what I've learned from yesterday :

_____
_____

DAILY PLANNER: Saturday

Date : _____
Sleep Hours : _____
Mood :

😞　　😟　　😐　　🙂　　😄
Very sad　Somewhat sad　Neutral　Somewhat happy　Very happy

Today I'm grateful for: _____

EXERCISE	TIME

BREAKFAST	LUNCH	DINNER	SNACK

Life lessons & what I've learned from yesterday :

_____

_____

DAILY PLANNER: Sunday

Date : _____
Sleep Hours : _____
Mood :

very sad | somewhat sad | neutral | somewhat happy | very happy

Today I'm grateful for: _____

EXERCISE	TIME

BREAKFAST	LUNCH	DINNER	SNACK

Life lessons & what I've learned from yesterday :

_____
_____

DAILY PLANNER: Monday

Date : _____
Sleep Hours : _____
Mood :

😞 😟 😐 🙂 😊
Very sad Somewhat sad Neutral Somewhat happy Very happy

Today I'm grateful for: _____

EXERCISE	TIME

BREAKFAST	LUNCH	DINNER	SNACK

Life lessons & what I've learned from yesterday :

_____
_____

DAILY PLANNER: Tuesday

Date : _____
Sleep Hours : _____
Mood :

😣   😟   😐   🙂   😊
very sad   somewhat sad   neutral   somewhat happy   very happy

Today I'm grateful for: _____

EXERCISE	TIME

BREAKFAST	LUNCH	DINNER	SNACK

Life lessons & what I've learned from yesterday :

_____

_____

DAILY PLANNER: Wednesday

Date : _____
Sleep Hours : _____
Mood :

😠 😟 😐 🙂 😄
very sad   somewhat sad   neutral   somewhat happy   very happy

Today I'm grateful for: _____

EXERCISE	TIME

BREAKFAST	LUNCH	DINNER	SNACK

Life lessons & what I've learned from yesterday :

_____
_____

DAILY PLANNER: Thursday

Date :
Sleep Hours :
Mood :

very sad   somewhat sad   neutral   somewhat happy   very happy

Today I'm grateful for:

EXERCISE	TIME

BREAKFAST	LUNCH	DINNER	SNACK

Life lessons & what I've learned from yesterday :

DAILY PLANNER: Friday

Date : _____
Sleep Hours : _____
Mood :

😞 😟 😐 🙂 😊
Very Sad Somewhat Sad Neutral Somewhat Happy Very Happy

Today I'm grateful for: _____

EXERCISE	TIME

BREAKFAST	LUNCH	DINNER	SNACK

Life lessons & what I've learned from yesterday :

_____
_____

DAILY PLANNER: Saturday

Date : _____
Sleep Hours : _____
Mood :

😟 😕 😐 🙂 😊
very sad   somewhat sad   neutral   somewhat happy   very happy

Today I'm grateful for: _____

EXERCISE	TIME

BREAKFAST	LUNCH	DINNER	SNACK

Life lessons & what I've learned from yesterday :

_____
_____

DAILY PLANNER: Sunday

Date : _____
Sleep Hours : _____
Mood :

😠 😟 😐 🙂 😊
Very Sad Somewhat Sad Neutral Somewhat Happy Very Happy

Today I'm grateful for: _____

EXERCISE	TIME

BREAKFAST	LUNCH	DINNER	SNACK

Life lessons & what I've learned from yesterday :

_____
_____